Words from my mind

by

Dale A. Dangleben, MD

Copyright © 2020 by Dr Dale Dangleben
All rights reserved. No part of this book may be reproduced, scanned, or distributed in any printed or electronic form without permission. Printed in the United States of America

DEDICATED TO MY BROTHER IAN BOWERS
LOVE YOU BRO

We are all but passing through this space and time - it gets hard sometimes - but we keep moving because time doesn't wait on us - sometimes memories are all we have - I will celebrate the great times ! - REST MY BROTHER

Table of Contents

Acknowledgement 7
Preface 9
SECTION 1..12
SECTION 2..36
SECTION 3..55

Acknowledgement

In this journey called life we meet so many influential people. Many times we don't get the chance to acknowledge them and say thank you. As a writer I want to take this opportunity in my book to say thank you to many.
Thank you to my mother and my father for believing in me. They instilled in me the foundation of what I ultimately became. My hunger for knowledge and wisdom and understanding came from my father. My mother always believed in me despite my wayward behavior as a young man. I firmly believe that my mother instilled in me my strength.
I must acknowledge my uncles and aunts especially Francis Warrington , who were there for me in my journey in the United States. I had food and shelter which was important parts of getting to the next phase to be better and greater.
There were many teachers who were influential in my life. There were many who did not have an impact because they were not devoted. That's OK because not everyone has what it takes. During my elementary school years I remember teacher Joycelyn and teacher Vilna Royer as model teachers. During my secondary education the devotion and commitment of Dr. Cuthbert Elwin and Brother Healy I shall never forget. I am forever

grateful because they introduced me to the sciences.

As we continue this journey, we meet people even those we meet for a very short time who takes the time to educate. I have knowledge all these educators. Many of us need mentors as we move along. During my medical school years Dr. Gordon Kaufman became a mentor while I worked in the laboratory during my residency, I was assigned a mentor. I did not like him. Looking back the person I would think will influence me during my training was Gary Nicholas my residency program director. I want to also acknowledge Dr. Peter Rovito An outstanding human being and mentor to me. To all those who took the time, I say thank you.

Even to those who were negative and out right racist I say thank you for opening my eyes to the reality of my surroundings

Dale A. Dangleben, MD

Preface

This inspiration to write comes from deep within me. We all have a message but we must find the time to deliver the message because time is not always on our side. The power of words should not be taken lightly. I have said many times I move fearlessly in the positive. The energy in the message most be positive in order to elevate. I have this responsibility to a generation to speak truth to power.

It is sometimes disheartening to see a generation going down a path so far from where they should be especially as a people. I call this hijacked faux black culture. The point is to be true to yourself and society as you move in this maze of time and try to uplift , even if its one person. There is always space for love . Loving yourself doesn't mean you hate someone else. Let us learn to love each other and enhance each other with this positive energy and not this stereotypes of negativity. Find yourself in the history books and change the rhetoric. Move away from the idea of violence and anger .

I write from deep within my mind and heart. If you think these words refer to you, then own it . Acceptance of flaws and deficiencies are important before stepping forward towards embracing positive change

I AM

I refused to be tamed nor contained ! Remember that strength is heart ,mind and soul - not muscle . No matter where I roam - proud to say that it is Scene city, Siboulie I came from ! Never forgetting brought west with the DNA of the earth - with the blood of Kings beyond time and understanding. Be the force of change of betterment and positivity to move forward – STAND AND BE COUNTED!

SECTION 1

CALL IT POETRY

THE CODE

You are
More than you think you are
The beginning ,
In the context of time
You are creation itself
Even before the Awash valley
In the Afar Triangle
Across the Oldvai Gorge
Stretch across the Serengeti
You are not Lucy in the Sky
But Dinknesh
The concept of DNA
You are it
From whence came Kings and Queens
Long before the Greeks and Romans
A time written off
Dismissed
As mythical
Find it
It's actually within you
You are a student in the library of Kemet
A king in the Empire of Mali
Millions of years you are
Yet a 2000 year concept defines you
Know yourself
You are the Moors of Spain and Sicily
Developed Europe
Yes that's all you
Sitted in the temple of Karnak

Right before the Roman invasion
Take a look at the Temple of Meroe
The Kingdom of Kush
You built that
How do I explain Timbuktu to you ?
Centers of Learning
Why don't you know of the Timbuktu
Manuscripts?
Yet speak of other scrolls found
You are migrating
To Asia and across the Bering Strait
Melanin decreased with time
A new phenotype
But you are there in the Genetic code
So you are Cherokee and Apache
Further south you are the Mayan architect
Aztec warrior you are
Long before Cortes and his yellow fever
So you see you are everything
what you are now
Was Forced on you
A guise of superiority and supremacy
The true superiority is in the code
Torn and beaten
Through the middle passage
Whipped and hung
Bent and not broken
Because you are still here
You are the blueprint
It's all in the code .

THE DRUMS

Do you still hear the drums
That rhythm that vibrates in the depths
of your soul
That finds you moving without even
thinking about it
Resonance of the time of freedom in
the cradle of civilization
Drums beating where people rose to
heights never known
You don't believe me
Ask Mansa
A time of intellect
A time of creation and development
An energy driven by earthly tones
translated in the beat of that drum
The drums of Africa
Stretched across the ocean through
time
Down mountains and across streams
Creating a vibration of survival
Forcing the chants to invoke the great
spirits of the earth
That kept us strong and a need to be
free
Gave us that fighting spirit
Yes the beat of the drum
That rhythmic pulsation of the drums
Is it fading?
Lost

Another part of the history stolen?
Taken into captivity and transformed
Into another source of oppression
Dancing to this new sound of a new
drum, of a new master
No longer a drum that echoes through
the ancestry
One of deception
A new beat that drowns the soul of
your royalty and distinction
A new sound of guns and banging of
prison cells
One of bribery with fame and fortune
That has disconnected you from your
history
If only you knew the true rhythm of the
drum
Then maybe just maybe you could
understand how great you are
We now march to a different beat
As the ancestral drums sinks
In the dark shadows of the Atlantic.

THE AGENDA

Sometimes we all find ourselves
fighting the darkness
The cancers of this society that we
think we should embrace
The anger and frustration
Driven by few
Those with power and an agenda
To Divide and conquer
Rule
As you find yourself crying
Look to the child
The seed of the future
And teach
Speak the truth
Forcefully
For while there is still hope
And a chance to love
Then there can still be harmony
Your today was generated
From the lessons of yesterday
Remember that this Obsession with
Race
Superiority or Supremacy
Was shaped by Man
Not Angels
No acknowledgment of where the
Race began
How will it end !
Who we all are

The True Genesis
Not Revelation
Look at the DNA of the earth
Knowledge and Wisdom
Words you can't pronounce
Australopithecus afarensis
Not me , then who
3 million years
No concept of time
Too greedy and selfish
Preaching of an afterlife
Downplaying the games played
In this evil playground
Acceptance of misogyny and nepotism
At the highest level
Proud Racist
Feeling like the Wizard
Owner of all sorcery
Here comes time to teach us again
Dust you came
In the end you will be
That particle in the wind

I AM HERE

Created from the broken pieces
That I once was
Put back together from strength and wisdom
Not violence as you claim
Am standing here
Sharp mind, firm feet
Willing to meet chaos
Where it meets me
Defend my existence
I exhale deeply
I am everything you told me
I could not be
I am everything that I told myself
I was going to be
Crawled out of the darkness
And became the light
Out of the shadows
Stepped bravely
Inhale deeply
Eagle eye see clearly
Not forgetting who I was
The coldest of winter
Now am that warm sun of summer
Shining
I once was that acorn
Begging for water
Now I am the oak
Standing tall

Am that raging waters of the river
Quenching the ocean
You see ....
I have become what you fear
Not the physical
But a mind so complex
Can't be contained
It keeps you up at night
Wishing I would go away
But I have just arrived
I'll be here
Sitting at your table
Learning my next move

THE CUP OF BLOOD

Racist you are
As you fill your cup
With the blood of my ancestry
Own it and accept it
Celebratory heroes
Perversed
Not mine
More I look the more i see
Stains of blood
Spirits still roaming
Not at peace
So I refuse to celebrate
Black bodies thrown overboard
Midatlantic

You are Leopold in the Congo
Heartless bastard
Chopping hands of my children
You are Hitler
Destroying the Jews
That fascist Mussolini
Gassing Ethiopia
You are Hawkins and Drake
Plundering and Murdering
High noon on the Atlantic
You are soldiers
At Wounded knee
With your Hotchkiss gun in hand
Massacring the Lakota Indians
Columbus the villain
Boasting " we could subjugate them all "
So he did
Ask the Arawaks
KKK riding and burning
Smell of my flesh
J Edgar Hoover
A Criminal minded fabricator
Framing my people
Dylaan Roof
Walking into a Charleston church
Columbine, Sandy Hook , Parkland
Now the Norm, a new culture
Grasping your gun
Pointed at Botham
Fire
Ignoring Garner screams

I can't breathe
Do you understand?
You are Trump
The Epitome of Misogyny
Acceptance of Nepotism
Anti hero coward
Racist you staring at me
Like you are better
Trust me you are not !

BE QUIET AND LISTEN

Greedy you are
Wrapped in jealousy
Confused soul
 Clouded mind
You look at yourself an empty shell in need of love
Your anger and jealousy masks your talent
Swimming in your puerility
Can't hear over your screams
The baby you are
Longing for a womb
To keep you safe
Can't control yourself
Maybe Need a leash
A handler
Keep you at bay
Know it all
No one better

I and me
All doors closed
Lack of understanding
 Your envy of others is a virus
Infecting your core
That Ego
Eroded by Freudians Id
Fighting yourself
Searching for a deeper gratification
Accept who you are
Reflect in silence
Listen to the whispers of the
Super Ego
Humility
Will guide you
You let you anger Lead
and your idea of wisdom
Crushed by raw ignorance
While your heart races
Your mind trying to catch up
You see
Not everyone has what it takes
Accept yourself

DICTATOR

Dictator You are
A tyrant against your own
Used your charm to get there
Think of the times

Not a penny to your name
Suit borrowed
Pants too long
Gratitude never shown
Pushing your bicycle
Restless sleep
Devising schemes
To get on top
Opportunity knocked
But a price they paid
Heart stopped
Just to sit on the throne
Memorandum of Understanding
Beginning of dirty secrets
Take the reporter
To court
How dare he
Accusations of acquisitions
Can't afford it
The country to know
Like a crack feign
The money burned your eyes
Easily tricked
While the Palm got greased
Circle of friends
Many for sale
Even across the pond
Hand stretched out
Big Apple condominium
Millions to spare
Curse of Macau lingers

Ask Ashe
Weighted down
Then the Persian
Passport peddler
Double agent
Hiding in plain sight
Catch him if you can
Yes the gingerbread man
See the once bicycle man
Rubbing elbows
Billions please
Champagne on ice
Never going back
Wealth beyond
The wildest dream
Oh you tyrant
Dictator you are
Vowed never to be poor
Even if it cost you
The entire country
Yes you child of a man
Dictator became
Can't even recognize yourself
Sad example for the children
Interestingly you see
History Never showed you
Dictators never win

A NEW DAY

You told me to be hopeful
You tell me to keep hope alive
Tell me about a pie in the sky
Told me to pray and hold on
That there is so much more for me
In the afterlife
While you drink and eat plenty
Sipping on your expensive wine
Staring at me under spectacle eyes
While I'm on my knees asking
Begging
Minimum wage I am
Despite all my efforts
Keep me crying
Tell me to turn to your image
Hanging on my wall
Not my hue, eyes blue
Want me on my knees
Pray for Forgiveness
But why do I need forgiveness
Was I the one who cracked the whip?
I was not the one who steered
the ship
 Middle passage
Pain beyond compare
You told me to read the good book
It will show me the path to
righteousness
Am looking around

Don't see your righteousness
Just an overgrown path of repetitive poison
Keys jingling
Jail cells clanking
Mothers still crying
Young boys dying
I want mine now
Just like you
Not in another time
Keep the caviar
I don't like it
I will take the wheel of my destiny
Lead my path
Earn and own my space
Where I can breathe
Without being choked on the side walk
Where I can walk with my hoodie
Live to see 20
Where I can sit peacefully in my home and watch TV
Bang Bang bleeding
Can you hear what am saying
Not asking
Am talking to you
Lower that cup of mocha latte
Dismissive you are
But It's a new day
Resurrection of kings and Queens
No more asking

The awakening is at hand
Fist in the air
Not palm out begging
No more !

BELIEVE IT

Can you believe
I was once a caterpillar and a butterfly
Can you believe
I was once an innocent child
Looking forward to a world of peace and happiness and understanding?
Can you believe
 I was once quiet and shy sitting in a corner by myself?
As I grow older I saw the world for what it was-a space of confusion and turmoil
Brought on by humanity itself,
I saw brothers against brothers and sisters fighting sisters,
The world of harmony
I dreamt of as a child did not exist,
I saw lies defined in written text
Sculpted by man designed as God,
I saw suffering of children because of cruelty and unscrupulous men,
I saw hunger and starvation from the
Shores of Haiti
To the depths of

Africa,
I saw greed and corruption
Where mankind had forgotten the value of
Love and forgiveness,
We pray and wait
For the coming savior
When it's up to each and everyone of us
To save humanity,
To find the silver lining in our hearts
The here and now
We must fix this world!

GO!

Hear their claps
Sounds of thunder
Echoes of laughter
Cheering at obscenity
So misdirected
Tainted heart
Misogynist
Blatant racist
Rhetoric of hate
Resonating
Lost followers yelling
Some Singing hymns
Mockery of position
No regard for anything
Selfish agenda
Nepotism defined

Lost soul you are
Oh great one
Hear the scream
Wake up
It's time for you
To go
You are fired !

WHERE IS MARCUS

Where are the great leaders who set
the path for the Caribbean?

The fearless men and women like
Bussa, Tula, Kofi, Jaco, Nanny,
Cudjoe, Bogle and Aponte. The rebels
against slavery - burn down plantations
to free their people

The revolutionary spirit of the greats
like Toussaint, Christophe, Dessalines
and Dutty Boukman - not even the
short egotistical maniac Napoleon with
his army could stop them.

The appreciation of our African-ness
like Marcus Garvey - I am still looking
for him in the whirlwind and the storm
to take me back to Africa.

The Greats like Eric Williams, Forbes Burnham, Walter Rodney, Cecil Rawle men of great intellect who understood the struggle against colonialism.

Let's not forget the great women like Elma Francois, Claudia Jones and Nanny. That African matriarchal energy they embodied, and they fought even in an era when they were told women had no right to

The times when our leaders were deeply spiritual and rooted in culture of Africa

Who is our Kwame Touré or our Frantz Fanon? Men of vision and willingness to stand for what they believed in.

We are left with a bed of corrupted leaders who are for self and sold us back into colonialism. Our ancestors are crying as our fake leaders are using rhetoric of inclusion while their action is that of suppression and oppression. No vision of African culture but with loyalty to China and Russia.

They have killed the dreams of the youths as the Caribbean becomes a basin of mendicancy. Leaders buy degrees instead of hard work a sad example for the children. They have turned to selling their birth rights to increase their financial worth. So, the youths turn and look for quick rewards and the epidemic of drugs and alcoholism washes at the shores of the West Indies.

I see Toussaint crying! I see Garvey crying! I see Nanny and Cudjoe crying.

Where are our strength to burn it all down to the ground again to start over?

May the Higher Power you believe in continue to guide the lost souls of the Caribbean

I step forward in the deepest of Garveyite consciousness

RACISM

I am not supposed to be
Where I am
The obstacles
The harassment
The torment

The weight to bear
It has all changed me
What have I gained
When I have lost
so much in the process
Of fitting in
Why do they feel
Intimidated
Define my assertiveness
As anger and aggression
I walk with my head up
My mother would be proud
Can't cut me down
Am confident
You are mad
Am not your puppet
So I must be brought down a notch
To listen to you
Yet you can't even look me in the eye
Am too strong for you
Maybe even too smart for you
Am not supposed to be here
Much less question you
Like a dog am supposed to
Stay
Speak only when spoken to
Am the orderly
Not the surgeon
But I live with integrity and love
Of all humanity

Your insecurity cannot take away from me
What my mother instilled in me
Does my voice offend you?
Maybe it's my cockiness
Am loud
But look deeper
Is it my skin color?
Or my Caribbean accent
Or that flair of confidence that hits your core
Because am not like you
Your hatred is yours
I don't claim it and don't want it
My compassion for the less fortunate
Is my guide
My moral compass
Not your spoiled privileged ways
You would not have lasted one day on my journey
I didn't have that privilege you have
I had to work harder and smarter
Even through the cries
Of affirmative action
You don't know me
So, don't pretend you do
You owe me an apology
I sacrificed here
For you
To reap the benefits
Yet you repay me

With discontent
And Racism
You are vile
Well my color doesn't define me
Money doesn't define me
My love for all humanity defines me
So, continue
With your racist self

FORBIDDEN PLACES

We are all vulnerable
With places in our hearts
We dare not go
Places destroyed by some
Moment of time in the past
Had to be buried
These moments to determine
How we love again
Or hurt again
Try not to hate again
So a place forbidden
Locked away in time
Trying never to remember that pain
A burning sensation never felt
A time of fear
When all you wanted was love
Lay your head calmly

With me where you
Now belong
Breathe a fresh air
Of the rebirth of love
Secure feelings
Locked in a Chest
Of precious memories
Somethings are meant to stay back
While others are meant to bloom in spring

SECTION 2

THE DOODLER

Recently, I found my mind drifting. In its creativity I began to doodle. It was almost therapeutic. The most came out when I was in a stressful situation. My pen would move on the paper even when multitasking. I would start with the simplest of imagery and grow it into something abstract. I wanted to share a few of these with you. You may interpret it as you wish because that's the whole point.

THE FACE
Let your face tell your story.

THE PRISONER
Many a times we become prisoners of our own minds that cripples the body and soul and deprives the self of success. Stay free.

CONFUSION
With all the noise and chaos around
you there is always a place for silence.
Find it.

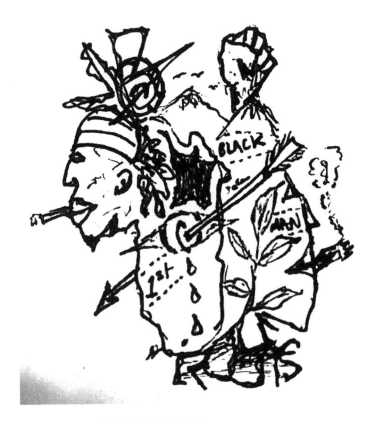

AFRICAN I AM
Be yourself and embrace your ancestry and understand the struggle especially of those who came before you

THE EYE THAT SEES
While you look outwards also look within, there is greatness there.

THE PUPA
Change is a constant as we move through time, embrace it and make it your own.

PRISONER OF YOUR MIND
The only prison is your mind that you make your oppressor – boundaries set forth by your own mind

CONTAINED

Don't get caught up by walls and obstructions set by those who want to see you fail. Start climbing.

FUSION
Things will come together if you work at it. Bring the talent and thoughts and love together and you will achieve great things

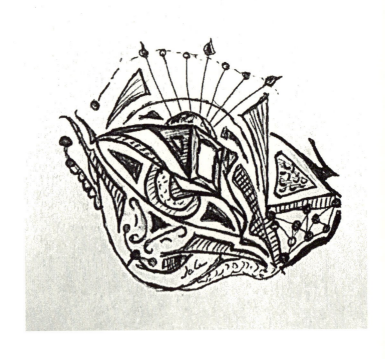

DIRECTION
Life may pull you in all directions but like a vector a sum of the forces will lead you

DIFFERENT
Its ok to be different as long as its not
in the negative. See things others
don't see because of your gift.
Embrace it

FACES
Sometimes what we put out is only a mask of the pain we feel inside. Fear not because the pain will subside so keep smiling

SAME
At the end of it all we are all the same,
from dust to dust so stop the hatred
and greed and start sharing

UNIQUE
Don't let anyone take away your uniqueness. Be whatever you want to be as long as its in the positive.

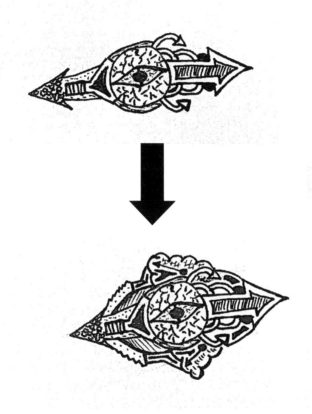

GROWTH
As time goes by continue to grow in your generosity and love for humanity. Keep your eyes open on the positive

LOVE
Even when there is pain and hurt let the love within you emanate and be your solace . Your love for others will be your comfort

DREAMING
There will be dark skies and rainy days
but think of the horizon and the rising
of the sun and all that beauty around
you and take it all in and make it yours

OF THE GRID

I drifted at my desk one day dreaming of my up bringing in Dominica. I longed for the days of just pure peace and innocence. But the greatness in that moment is that it still lives within me and in my mind as I drew what I felt was peaceful.

SECTION 3

FEARLESSLY FREE IN THE POSITIVE

TEARS

We feast on plenty while the rivers of the Caribbean run dry and the children are dying of thirst – thirst of wisdom, thirst of understanding of self and history. They are surrounded by greed and left with a feeling of hopelessness. I weep for them

FIND MARCUS

Be aware and READ more - it sparks a fire in your heart and mind to understand history and even the manipulation of history . I read about Marcus Mosiah Garvey passionately. This is a man we should not forget . Find Marcus and his writings and be his whirlwind and his storm . I created this shirt to celebrate the man and even if I shouldn't have to tell you but please " REMEMBER MARCUS" - Long live Marcus and all the greats of the Caribbean . It's up to us to carry that legacy and never let it die .

KEEP CLIMBING

As I always say haters will hate it's their nature. Don't be stagnant in your climb even when you encounter the snakes on the climb . What's success without challenge? Also be cognizant of the traps set to take you down - look out for envy and jealousy they are closer to you than you think . Don't let anyone steal your shine . Your strength is built on all the weaknesses and hardships you have survived- keep moving and stay strong ! The garbage your enemy throws at you is a reflection of their state of mind.

MY LIFE

I crawled then stood and I walked then I ran and on the shoulders of my ancestors I grew wings to take flight . I am everything that has haunted me and bent me along this journey but never broke me and out of weakness came strength . I have mistaken dusk for dawn and in fogs of illusion kept looking for solutions to problems that could not be solved . Peace lies in understanding that - and knowing that not every challenge is worth fighting for - live and love your life with open options and don't let anyone steal your light Stay blessed

KNOW YOUR SELF WORTH

Walk with your head up and if the load is heavy and the back is aching - walk with a big stick "
Find yourself amidst the chaos
A pocket of silence
Extract the noise
Be at peace with yourself
Be the keeper of your destiny
And the captain of your journey
Don't let the haters hate on you
Shine forward
And Rise .

ROAD LESS TRAVELLED

Easy roads, short cuts and shortsightedness leads to pain and sorrow in the end . Hard work and sacrifice defines the destiny and calms the heart in the appreciation of the accomplishment . I will reiterate, I am standing on the shoulders of my mother and father and those before them , my ancestors . This journey brought me to a point of finding true self despite the deliberate obstacles . The metamorphosis is complete - time is my keeper ! Your opinion of me no longer matters - it's yours , you can keep it. As much as you would love to retract my accomplishment it's mine - you can't take it !! Cant you see am fanon , Garvey, Malcolm, Martin and far back to Akhenaten ? Still I roam ....

DON'T BE CONFUSED

ITS A NEW DAY - ONE OF BRAVERY AND NEED TO BE FEARLESSLY FREE IN THE POSITIVE . Loving yourself does not mean you hate another . Don't let anyone make you think that . But first you must stop the hatred of self . We each need to wake up in the deepest of Garveyite consciousness. This is no joke , people are dying as we use social status, religion and politics to divide us while the oppressors uses our own to control the narrative on what our culture and way forward should be . Marcus Garvey led by example started a path to economic independence and because of that vision they destroyed him and many after him . We sit in confusion hating each other and jealous of each other with no bargaining power . We give all earnings back to the machinery that oppresses us . We put our money in banks that hesitates to give us loans . We shop in stores where they follow us around thinking we are all there to steal . We buy billions in weaves and shoes and don't own any . It's up to each and everyone of us to change the rhetoric and action towards the collective upliftment . It's not about hatred of others but about love of self . It's time to love and trust each other .

NO CONTROL

Those who think they control the key to the gate of other's success are fools . Only Time is the keeper and controller of destiny. Freedom of mind and heart is the key to your path . So those who see themselves as egomaniacs trying to control and manipulate others what will you do when Father Time meets you at his gate ? Open your eyes and see what's before you and speak and act from deep within and leave superficialities alone . As for me I move in the deepest of consciousness of Marcus Mosiah Garvey .

CHOP IT DOWN

I saw the slithering snake with it's forked tongue trying to get into the chicken coop........ it's a shame it did not see the cutlass on the wall , sharpened and ready to cut it down

EMPTY BARRELS ROLLING

The words of men without action are like a basket with water - it can't be filled - many men have chosen to walk dangerous roads in hope of enrichment of self. With an eye of destruction of others they destroy themselves- When you transcend materialism then your basket will be filled with plenty - so those who chose to play with fire may just get burned . I have chosen the road less traveled and learning to give instead of taking and grabbing everything - remember this " sticks and stones break bones" but words of a fool further defines him/her in their echo chamber of stupidity."! We are our own worse enemies like crabs trying to get out of a barrel while our master has the stick shoving us back in .Narrow minded people focus on people while great minds implements ideas. Jealousy and envy serves evil so choose your master carefully or else you are a slave again - Watch me roam and learn

REBIRTH

I AM AKHENATEN
I AM IMOHTEP
I AM MANSA
I AM NEG MAWON
I AM NANNY
I AM MARCUS
I AM ELMA
I AM NKRUMAH
I AM MALCOLM
I AM MARTIN
I AM KWAME
I AM MANDELA

YES I AM

It's not just about talk but action .
Action to enlightenment and upliftment
. I have embraced my calling and plan
on continuing this education of our
people . The damage to the Caribbean
should be a concern for all of us -
LONG LIVE THE NEG MAWON

NOT AN OPTION

Never allow yourself to be an option
Always think and be at least two steps
ahead
Embrace your greatness and your gift
no matter what it is - Not too many
may even understand you- Don't be
forsaken or frustrated
So much so that you allow others to
dim your light and define your
existence.

KEEP SHINING........

Be content in your path but be
cautious , there are snakes in the
grass on the edge of this path . Be
careful who you call your friend,
because not everyone wants to see

you climb , some may sit with you and laugh with you but don't want you in that circle, join the laughter but don't drink the wine , it's saturated with hate and envy . Always look within , there are answers there - no need to follow the crowd . First and foremost find yourself and love yourself and I assure you the forgiveness of your enemies will be easier . Don't be jealous of others and their worldly gains - there is more in giving and helping the less fortunate than always having your hands out and taking . Do good and you will be rewarded tenfold . As for me am still here taking this slow walk in the house of exile.

SAVE A LIFE

Many sit in the judgement of others because of race , color and creed - consumed with their own misery and shortsightedness spending time fighting each other - over the last 20 years in medicine I have seen the best of humanity but trust me I have seen the diabolical side to our humanity- the violence and hate - despite all this as trauma surgeons, we fight to save everyone with the goal of functional survival. I often reflect on this journey and have accepted the dichotomy of mankind - the key is to always do good and minimize the bias and truly treat others as you would want to be treated especially when on the brink of death .

REFLECT

Always reflect on where you are no matter good times or bad times , it will allow for readjustment to satisfaction and see your surroundings for what it is , negative or positive. If you are not content look for better but more importantly be at harmony with yourself- you are made up of everything you have endured and survived to be stronger - we all have two sides it's up to us which one dominates . Remember those who waste time and energy trying to bring you down are not cerebrally or spiritually developed to comprehend innovation, creativity or erudition-leave that behind

SHAME ON YOU

You may sit in your silence today
maybe even in prayer asking for
forgiveness of sins of triviality when
the main travesty you support is the
ultimate evil and this despotic fool who
has ICE agents running AMOK as you
sit silently hoping they will rid you of
your historic guilt , as you sit in
privilege of inherited circumstance
sipping on your Argentinian Malbec
and tasting your medium rare Kobe
beef or maybe Hershey hot chocolate
from Ghanaian cocoa beans or your
Columbian coffee or your swanky
Quinoa salad from the Andes
mountain of Bolivia - you bloody
hypocrite - how quick you forgot you
too are an immigrant - yes you - if not
you then your grandparents - how dare
you point fingers. Open a book and
read on history and where you came
from and how you ended up here . I
find too many of you don't even know
who America is named after or that
Columbus never stepped foot on
mainland much less anything deeper .
Instead you argue about things you
have no understanding
and instead spew the rhetoric of the

1% who keeps us in a perpetual state of division and confusion to ensure their continued success . The reality is you have lost your identity also and it bothers you about this new conglomeration- GET USE TO IT

ENRICHMENT

The strength of being free is to be fearless ! Not in terms of violence and negativity but fearless towards inspiring, uplifting and enhancing not just yourself but those around you ! Enrich yourself with wisdom and pass it on . Surround yourself with people of integrity- those who focus only on self enrichment of material things will not be content inside .

HYPOCRITE

As you sit in your congregation with a mentality of segregation thinking you are better than the other with your hatred and hypocrisy , don't you think for a minute you are burning in this hell you believe in ? Love is love and you can't redefine it to suit your selfish agenda - so sit there with the book in your hand repeating words that comforts your heart yet still you can't love your neighbor, can't clothe your brother and can't feed your sister - keep your hypocrisy- I'll keep walking towards the exit of the house of exile .

HATERS HATE

Haters will always hate so let them hate - keep moving , stay focus on where you are going but enjoy the scenery as you go by , subtract the negative energies they are not worth your time . Despite what many may think most people don't want to see you get ahead even many who are close to you - they are slithering creatures with evil intent so know them for who they are . Find inner peace it will be your greatest achievement.

Forgive them for they know not what they have done !! God bless the warriors ! The Neg Mawon !

YOUR PRISON

The only prison is your mind that you have now made your Oppressor. It's not the past or present . You are your limitation despite that external pressure . There are no boundaries, but the ones set forth by your own mind. Free your mind . Look forward .

CORRUPT YOU

I walk these days in the deepest of Garveyite Consciousness and speak against the evil that corrupt politicians and so call leaders are doing . They scream democracy while they sleep in beds of dictatorship and enriching themselves at the expense of the people . Their organizations are digging their own grave . They are corrupting their nations just because they are greedy . The courts are bought and they are changing laws in their favor to buy elections and keep the poor poorer. A generation will be lost if we the people don't intervene .

THE STAIN

This cloud of hatred and injustice that cast a shadow around us is such a stain on our humanity . I embrace this peace I found in places I never thought to look. Find your better self

FEARLESS

The strength of being free is to be fearless! Not in terms of violence and negativity but fearless towards inspiring , uplifting and enhancing not just yourself but those around you .

REFLECTION

It is ok to get lost .It's about finding your way back. Back to peace and confidence . See the mistakes of the past . Your restless mind led by a wayward heart. Was just a torment of youth now turned into reflection of self. Brings a smile and warmth because time has given you that opportunity to learn from your mistakes.

ENHANCEMENT

Be judged by the content of your character and by what you do for others without wanting anything in return. Walk with your head up with confidence . Let your mind and heart work in harmony. Don't stress over trivialities just do great work and enhance your talents and gifts for the betterment of humanity.

BE KIND

When your heart and mind connects , this idea of humanity MUST prevail. Be wise in all you do . Be kind even to those you know hates you. Show your depth . Lend a hand to those who fights against you but keep away from the knife- don't let it get to your back " Et tu Brute"

LET IT RAIN

Sometimes ,time is like torrential tears that rolls down your cheek that washes away at your feet but that's okay because after the tears will be laughter, peace and joy.

ITS MINE

My enlightenment and wisdom and the understanding of who I am in this space and time is the greatest freedom I have that makes me fearless. You can take my wealth and all things material but this awakening is something that can't be taken from me – Its woven in my heart and soul.

BE WOKE

On the shoulders of the ancestors I stand – freedom of mind and spirit. Those who sit in conspiracies and jealousy stand in their own way solely based on an inferiority mentality- embracing individuality even in the collective makes us better. So to each his own just don't let that internal flame lead to spontaneous combustion. Remember Marcus – and what he wanted for us- " Up ye mighty race"- get out of the barrel.

MY TABLE ALSO

You did not invite me to the table , but I sat down anyway and I ate and drank while you looked at me with suspicious eye. You steaming inside to see me there enjoying the ambiance, seeing my brilliance just frustrates you just because of an idea you were thought. Think about that.

ACCEPT THE STORM

Let it rain and let the wind blow. Let the storms rage against you , stand strong, always fight likes its your last fight , life is sometimes about the storms and getting through them, so when the storm is gone you can do your best work.

GIVE MORE

Don't take – Give!
That's what it's about
Penance and repentance
The love for humanity
The shirt of your back
To you brother
About loving another
If you cant share and give back
Then there is no purpose

FORGET NOT THYSELF

Too many times we forget ourselves and give so much of us to others that we forget the real reason for the journey. You are the limitation to your happiness ,Drop the fears of yesteryear and take a chance.

RACING MIND

Sometimes your thoughts are scattered and blown like the dust and tumbleweed on a hot desert day – wondering where it will stop. Keep the thoughts going and write a book.

GARVEY
Movements of our people in terms of pride in who we are despite the middle passage and the suffrage. The need for an awakening of that consciousness.

One of the greatest gifts that my father ever gave me were books. Books became the seed of my wisdom and my curiosity to find out more about this world around me. The right books can be the gateway to open your imagination to bigger and greater things. Because of reading, I sought a deeper knowledge of self. Now, I have come full circle to understand who I am in context of history as a black man. I look to the future with a greater understanding of my history and those who carved a way for me. Up ye mighty race!

Made in the USA
Middletown, DE
14 April 2022